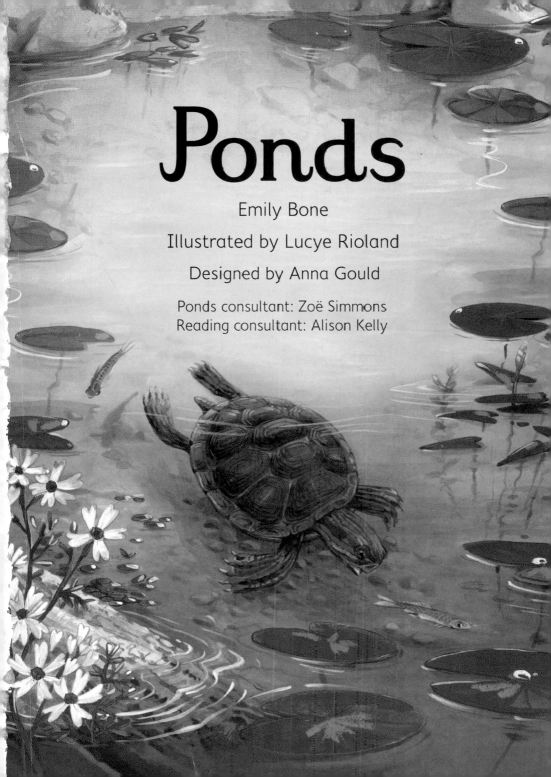

Ponds

Emily Bone

Illustrated by Lucye Rioland

Designed by Anna Gould

Ponds consultant: Zoë Simmons
Reading consultant: Alison Kelly

Lots of different plants and
animals live in ponds.

Dragonflies and damselflies
fly above the water.

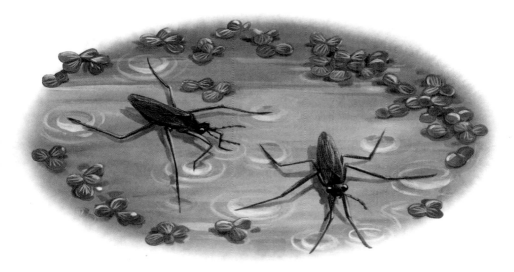

Water striders balance on the surface.

Fish swim at the bottom of ponds.

Many plants grow in ponds.

Water mint

Water weed grows completely underwater.

Water lilies float on
the surface.

Water
violet

Fish shelter
among the plants.

Ponds are home to lots of different fish.

Father stickleback fish look after their babies.

Some fish have flowing fins and tails.

Others have short ones.

Some pond animals are fierce hunters.

Great diving beetles dive down to catch fish.

Water scorpions grab animals to eat.

Whirligig
beetle

Young dragonflies are called nymphs.
They have long jaws to catch food.

Tadpole

Jaw

A dragonfly nymph climbs up a plant.

Nymph

Suddenly, its skin splits. An adult dragonfly climbs out...

...and flies away to
find food.

Dragonflies and damselflies
dart around hunting bugs.

Hawker
dragonfly

This dragonfly
is hunting a
mayfly.

Common blue
damselfly

Some stop to rest
on plants.

Scarlet darter
dragonfly

13

Frogs, toads and newts come to
ponds in spring to lay eggs.

Great crested
newts

They lay tiny
white eggs
on leaves.

14

Frogs and toads call to find partners.

American toad

Trill trill trill!

This frog makes a peeping call.

Peep peep!

Frogs lay lots of eggs,
called frogspawn.

Tiny tadpoles hatch
out of the eggs.

Tadpoles grow back legs...

...and then front legs.
They get bigger too.

Croak!

Finally, they turn into frogs.

Pond snails crawl up and down underwater plants.

They eat leaves.

Fish and frogs
hunt the snails.

19

Water spiders live in ponds.

A spider traps air from the surface between hairs on its body.

It dives down and builds a web
between pond plants.

It fills the web with the air and climbs inside. The spider breathes the air.

A young mosquito passes close by. The spider rushes out to catch it.

Turtles lie in the hot sun at edges of ponds to warm up.

They have hard shells.

They can hide away inside their shells.

They slide into the cool water
to hunt for food.

Plop!

Mayflies grow up underwater in ponds.

When they're ready to turn into adults, they come to the surface.

24

They fly in big groups looking for partners.

Can you spot something else hiding in the pond?

Many different birds live around ponds.

Moorhens build nests at the edges of ponds.

Swallows snatch bugs off the surface.

Herons catch fish from under
the water.

Water shrews live in
burrows close to ponds.

They go to ponds to
hunt for fish and
beetles to eat.

A mother water shrew carries
a fish back to her burrow.

She feeds the fish to her babies.

29

Some ponds dry out
when it's hot and sunny.

When it rains, they fill
up with water again.

After the rain, lots of animals
come to live in the ponds.

Frog

Beetle

Tadpoles

Newt

31